Lost Identity

This is my story ...

Lost Identity

This is my story ...

Janice M. Gorden

Milwaukee, Wisconsin

Copyright © 2016 by Janice M. Gorden
All rights reserved.

Published by
Radiant Heart Press
An imprint of HenschelHAUS Publishing, Inc.
www.henschelHAUSbooks.com

ISBN: 978-1-59598-477-7
E-ISBN: 978-1-59598-478-4
Library of Congress Control Number: 2016941413

Printed in the United States of America

This book is dedicated to my dear sister, Jackie. I can't remember how many times I kept telling her, "You can't keep being so nice to people." But that is just who she was. Picking up people she didn't know and giving them rides and giving people food and money.
"What's wrong with you?" I'd say.
She would usually respond, "God told me to."

On her deathbed, she praised God out loud, then silently. After that, she stopped breathing.

I love you, Jackie.
Thank you for pointing the way.

Table of Contents

Acknowledgments 1

Introduction: My Story 3
My Encounter with God 14

Chapter One: Stick a Fork in Me; I Am Done 17
    Strength to Forgive 18
    "I am done." 18
    Giving Forgiveness, Gaining Closure:
    To Jethro (a 70-year-old man) 22

Chapter Two: Dragging Our Past into the Future 23
    Finding Freedom by Releasing Pain 24

Chapter Three: Splat 27
    God's Job at the Potter's Wheel 28
    Our Job on the Potter's Wheel 29
    Giving Forgiveness, Gaining Closure: To Joe 32

Chapter Four: Prayer Changes Things 35
    Expect a Change 36
    The Great Supper 37
    The Banquet and Us 40
    Old Things are Passed Away 41

Chapter Five: Big-Girl Moves 45
    Not a Garbage Can 47
    Chapter Six: Measure it up 49
    Bigger than God? 49
    Moving Forward 51
    Giving Forgiveness, Gaining Closure:
    To Otis (a 34-year-old man) 53

Chapter Seven: Perception of a Situation 55
   As a Man Thinks 56
   Making Up Stories 57
   Don't Jump to Conclusions 58
   That One Doesn't Count 59
   Don't be Pressured in Conversations 60

Chapter Eight: When I Get Stuck 63
   Keep Your Mind 64
   Perfect Peace 65
   My Peace 66
   Test the Spirit for Truth 67

Chapter Nine: Oscars vs Piranhas 69
   The Oscars 70
   Giving Forgiveness, Gaining Closure:
   To Clarence (a 15-year-old boy) 72

Chapter Ten: Blessed Assurance 73
   A Saving Relationship 73

Chapter Eleven:
Are you the One or shall I look for Another? 77
   Being 100% 81
   What Now? 84
   Spirit-Body-Soul 87
   Physical Health 88
   Spiritual Health 89

Closing: We Are Survivors 91

About the Author 97

Acknowledgments

Mother Kat spent a lifetime worth of energy telling how to live "saved." In her small bedroom, toward the end of her life, when I was supposed to be caring for her, she was caring for me. She would tell me repeatedly, "If you say something behind a person's back, be ready to say it to their face. Otherwise, don't say it," or, "When you mess up, be woman enough to fix it." She had many wise sayings, but nothing was like watching her live it. I watched her closely even though no one told me to. Mother Kat was saved inside and out. I love you, Mother Kat. When you left, I didn't believe I could live without your telling me what to do and how to do it. Mother Kat, you would be very proud of what you put in me. I proudly carry the mantle you gave me. I miss you.

My husband and partner, Charles, who loves me like none other. If I composed a list of all the qualities of those who have loved me before, that list would be nothing compared to Charles. Charles sticks by me. When I announced to him in

2001 that I was writing a book, he encouraged me. Afterward, I announced it again in 2007 and then in 2008, his response was the same. Baby, God gave me the words. I've been writing all the time. I adore you. Don't stop praying for me.

My mother, my BFF. I don't know how you took care of all of us, but you did. You did your best and we are the proof. Rest, Mama. As much as I miss you, rest.

Above all, I thank God for the life He gives me. Without Him, my blemishes show. Because of You, Lord, even with the blemishes You accept me. Not life nor death, height nor width ... nothing will separate me from the love of God through Christ. Your love has been my breath.

—Janice Gorden

Introduction: My Story

It is not what you say but what you do that is your signature. For the talkers, walk. For the walkers, talk. This book is not for everyone, just the ones who need to know God will take your curse and bless it.

This is a true story. Maybe some of the names were changed to protect others and maybe not.

No story told begins at the very beginning. I will begin my story with my mom.

She lived in Mississippi with her husband, who was twice her age. She moved away from him with my older two siblings to Milwaukee. She said he beat her up a lot. By the time Mom was 31 years old, she had 13 children. I am the fourth of those 13. Our father was married and had another family.

I remember the day Mama brought the last two children home, a boy and a girl. My eldest sister cried and said, "Every time Mama goes away, she comes home with more children."

I was "old-spirited." That is different from what some people call an "old soul." Nothing like that. My spirit felt old before my time because the young spirit had been taken from me early. It was normal for me to be molested or fondled any day any time. Some days, it was the old, gray-haired landlord that walked with a hunch. He smoked cigars and never seemed to shave. I can still taste the cigar tongue he put in my mouth and the scratches on my face from his beard.

Why me? I asked this for so many years afterward. Sometimes the question still arises from the child inside me. Was there a "rape me" tattoo on my forehead? How did they know?

I was six when things started happening to me. My cousins, my father, and by the age of 15, four different men had "had their way" with me. They were all "family" except one. I looked at families from shows like *Leave it to Beaver* and *The Huckstables* (with Cliff & Claire) in awe. I had no idea that families like that really existed in real life. My life was more like that of Sophia in *The Color Purple*.

I heard somebody say the ones who are least watched are the most vulnerable. That might be true. With 13 of us, my mom couldn't have been expected to watch us all. But that didn't help. It didn't comfort me or keep me safe.

What did I do to deserve to have my entire childhood taken away? Nothing was innocent anymore at an age that I should have been full of

Introduction

innocence and wonder. Why wasn't someone saving me out of this? I asked the question time and again. Even though I never told Mom, I couldn't understand why she didn't help me. Silent screams and invisible tears consumed me.

I wanted all my dresses long and my pants loose, not tight. But when there are 13 children, you have no choice of wardrobe. See, Mama? That's why they kept touching me, because they could see me. No help, no hope.

My cousin, who lived upstairs, offered me a quarter. He pulled me into the house and got on top of me. Today, I can figure out why he hurt me so very badly. He was a young teenager. As a child, though, I could not for the life of me figure out what he poked into me that was so painful. The old man wasn't that painful, but my cousin would not get off me. I cried and he held me down until he was finished. Then he gave me the quarter to shut up.

In the 1960s, I could take a quarter to the store and buy three bags of chips, a candy bar, and a popsicle. It wasn't a fair trade for innocence, but when you're in a family of 13 and the only provider is Mom, you know she is not going to give all of us a quarter. So I didn't tell anyone.

For the rest of his life, I made sure I wasn't found alone with that cousin. Right now, as I write this, I admit that he terrified me. This is the first time I ever said he scared me. I didn't hate him. I went to his funeral a few years ago, but I didn't feel a thing about him dying. I wasn't glad, nor was I sad.

Mama's grandma had children and one of her grandma's children married, so I guess that means he was technically another cousin through marriage, not really a blood cousin. He was a jokester in public, but what he did to me behind closed doors when I was eight years old wasn't funny at all. His front teeth were missing and he had a huge smile. He nauseated me nauseated. My underpants were always soaked afterwards; I hated him and what he did to me.

I didn't know I could tell grownups to stop hurting me. The 1960s were an era that children do not talk back to grownups. If a grownup said you did or didn't do something, that person was always right. I had to survive the best way I could.

I hated 5th Street. That house was full of roaches and cat-sized rats. Our nanny, Miss Annie, would put bacon on the mouse traps. Metal can tops covered the holes on the floor, where we often cut our feet. The house was immaculately cleaned daily. That's not why roaches lived there. It was just where they resided. The roaches lived there before we did, along with the rats. Then we moved in.

I soon found out that the best way to avoid being carried away by some grown-up to the attic upper flat or the neighboring house was to stay out of the back hall and the backyard. That's where they lurked, prowling, smiling with no teeth in front, golden yellow teeth, or cigar breath. For me, molestation was not unusual. It was a normal day. How could that be normal?

By some miracle, a neighboring pastor gave Mama the deed and paperwork to a house out of the "Hood." We moved away from the perverts in December of 1965. We didn't have much of anything to put in the house, but we were clean and I could breathe.

Miss Annie didn't come with us, and I knew I was going to miss her rice pudding. In the new neighborhood, everybody was Caucasian. Not another African American for a mile's radius in any direction.

The new school had two other African American families. Of course, they were our best friends until we got comfortable speaking clearly and precisely, like the Caucasian families. We learned other cultures and new habits, and went over our new friends' homes.

One of the neighbors also had a large family and would often bring cases of food and clothes to us. We didn't wear many of the clothes, but Mama said, "Take what is given you and say thank you," so that's what we did.

How Mama took care of all of us I haven't got a clue. After living in that home for over ten years, I saw Mom's paycheck stub. She made a little over $300 every second week. As we all got older, we helped her with bills, but she was never concerned with them out loud. I think our electricity was turned off once. My older brother had it reconnected when he worked at AO Smith.

Life was better there.

My father continued to come around like he lived with us, but Mama wasn't bringing any new babies home now. One day, he offered to take me somewhere. That was a treat because he did nothing for any of us, except sometimes one of my older sibs.

Once we were alone, he raped me. I just let him. I couldn't believe this was happening again. I thought I was safe. I let him do it several times more before I told him to stop it. He did stop, but even when he was 93, he continued to ask for sex from me. Depressed, wanting to die but too scared to kill myself, I lived my life.

How does a child recover her childhood? Once you eat the peach, how can the pit go back? I hated myself, my life, and my father.

Introduction

Depressed, my favorite color was black. I wore my dresses as long as possible, and wore them as often as possible, until Mama hid them from me. My breasts were larger than my oldest sister's. I was awkward, with a face full of pimples that I nervously broke open.

I was considered a bad girl in school. I kept fighting clothes in my locker at all times, just in case my older sister made me jump somebody at school. I don't remember why I beat up so many people, except for the fact my sister said, "if I didn't, she would beat me up." I thought all family relationships were like that.

All through school, I never failed a class. Of course, "D" was a passing grade. I put no effort into my class work. I was considered smart in grade school and sold my math papers for nickels.

For the most part, though, I hung out with the tough crowd, so I thought. One day, our tough gang of girls went to another school with the idea of fighting a group of girls who had been giving our girls a hard time. When we arrived at that school and saw the size of those girls, we turned right around and headed back to our own school, using the same transfer on the bus.

I thought of myself as a bad kid, one of the originals. It was nothing to fight a teacher or go into a classroom and start a fight with a student.

You could find me any day drinking Ripple in the park, smoking cigarettes and marijuana. Along with some of the girls, I snorted heroin, took acid, shot up tees and blues in my arm, but I didn't die. Once, I was given pills that made me sleep for two days, but I woke up.

I was 15 when I told my boyfriend I was pregnant. He left me. I didn't mind that so much. I did not want anyone to take care of my son except me.

My personality developed around these events in my life. By this time, I had no self-esteem. I hated myself, and would have welcomed death if it came my way. I was too scared to kill myself.

It was the very act of having children early that I believe saved my life. Lamont (my son) made me want to live—not for me, but for him. But it still didn't give me self-esteem, or make me love me, nor could I really let anyone else love me.

Many times, I still wanted to die, but at least I had someone to live for. My son saved my life. Lamont loved me and he thought I knew everything. His father had another child in January, after my son was born in November. I didn't care. This child was mine, and my mom didn't abandon me.

In June of 1975, I graduated from high school at 16 and a half years old.

Introduction

The next twenty years, I spent being beaten and robbed, drugging and drinking. I married a crack addict. I passed a nursing class and got a diploma. I went on to obtain an associate's degree in nursing. It made Mom so proud.

I was still as depressed as ever. It was the story of my life. It was who I was and since the time I was a child, I knew nothing else. Yet life went on. I lived it the best that I could with the knowledge I had obtained.

I believed God was God. I didn't grow up in church, even though my grandfather was a preacher.

At age 30, I started walking toward God. I took baby steps. Smaller than baby steps most times, if that is possible. I remember telling someone who criticized my walk to not take away the little I had. I talked to therapists and had to take antidepressants a few times to keep the smile on my face that people saw. I finally first spoke the incidents out loud at a women's conference years later, and the healing began.

I loved God and believed He would do great things for the people who are called by His name, but at the same time, I thought I was a lost cause. God delivered me from so many addictions, hangovers and hang-ups that I couldn't count them if I tried.

I grew in each church that I attended. A woman of God I knew as "Mother Kat" took me under her wings and placed me in many classes. Under her mentoring, I learned how to study, research the Bible, and pray for myself.

My second husband took me to another church where I learned to hang in there and how to let the Holy Spirit do the work. I began to catch the idea of wanting to work hard for the vision of the pastor, and the finances of the church. I learned how to lead in ministry. Most of all, the pastor taught me that when someone says something to you that hurts, it doesn't hurt as much as time passes.

I grew in the Lord, but I was still depressed. I was often on antidepressants, because my past was still my present. I had not dealt with my past. My personality was one of a six-year-old abused child. Was I called by His Name? Absolutely. I just didn't know what that meant or how to claim it completely.

When my mother passed away, I lost it. My mother had been my "bestest friend in the entire world." She was the "let's." I was the "go." I had brought her to our home (while in a coma) with me and my husband, and she passed away in my arms. It was storybook beautiful. Peaceful. Mom loved God. But I lost it.

Introduction

I tried to keep the smile. I wore the long-sleeve, turtleneck maxi-dresses. I spoke the words, and kept the emotions hidden in my heart. People could see I was alive, but I was dead. My husband had to talk me into wanting to live. I took antidepressants to smile, but I was a zombie. Was I called by His Name? Absolutely. But if you had asked, and if I had spoken the truth, I would have called myself anything but a beloved child of God.

I'm telling you this story so I can show you the glory that is in God. I took myself away from all I knew and was. I left that church. I didn't go back to my old church either; didn't go to church at all for that period in my life.

Church couldn't help me, to be honest. Not then. I needed the God of Abraham, Isaac, and Jacob, and I knew it. My back was against the wall and the only way I could move forward again was if I met with God Himself.

I questioned Him and His Word. "Lord," I said, "this is where the rubber meets the road. Like John said, "Are you the Messiah or shall I look for another?"

I called Him on every word He had ever given me. I called Him on scripture, and He taught me with a different understanding. I searched the scriptures for life, my Life.

As time passed, I realized that my back was no longer against the wall. My breath came easier. I depended on Him alone.

MY ENCOUNTER WITH GOD

I went on a weekend excursion with my new church. They referred to it as an "Encounter with God." This weekend was designed by a saved, sold-out therapist who created it for that very purpose: an Encounter with God.

Since then, I have not taken another antidepressant. Sometimes I go back to volunteer administer to others. I believe in it so deeply, because on that weekend, I had an encounter with God.

God Himself took me into His own arms and cared for me because I asked. God loves me. He tutored me. For the first time in my life, a certain fact came alive for me. I had "known" it in my head, perhaps, but not my heart. Now, the truth is unshakeable. What is that truth?

I am loved.

I am loved and I know it. I am worth loving. He has redeemed me. He has forgiven me. I'm not guilty.

Over time, my identity changed.

Introduction

I'm not 6, 8, or 14 anymore. That little girl is gone and I cannot base my life on what happened, but what was caused to happen.

When I looked at God for the first time, I was angry. How could an almighty God stand aside and let horrible things happen to innocent people? To children?

It took me a long time to come to terms with the truth. The reality is that I wouldn't be who I am today if I had not lived through the abuse. God didn't make them abuse me. They were evil, sick people. I didn't cause it to happen, either. I was just a child, but God took the very thing that should have killed me and made me glorify Him in it.

Crazy, huh? It might seem so, but I know that there are things I have learned, things that I have experienced, that will be a blessing to others only because of all that I have gone through. Perhaps you are one of those people. Perhaps you are struggling to find the strength to forgive, or the ability to move on, or the power to bring closure to a painful episode in your past. If that is who you are, I pray this short book will be a companion on your journey.

In the following pages, you will read some of the lessons God gave me to give others. Interspersed throughout, you will find short letters I have written to those who had hurt me the deepest. I feel that speaking these words of forgiveness are steps toward closure. Steps toward God. Though only words, I feel that something in them is doing something within me, recreating me in the image of God's Son, in whose name and by whose grace I write.

—Janice Gorden

Chapter One

Stick a Fork in Me; I Am Done

Let all bitterness, and wrath, and anger, and clamour, and evil speaking, be put away from you, with all malice: And be ye kind one to another, tenderhearted, forgiving one another, even as God for Christ's sake hath forgiven you. (Ephesians 4:31-32)

A few weeks ago, a good friend asked to borrow some money. Immediately, I went to the bank and dropped it off, expecting the return in a few days as my friend promised. A few days passed. No return. Money has been tight since my husband was unemployed. I needed the money reimbursed. I texted my friend a few times and got no response. I called and got no answer.

This had never happened before. I didn't want to let it affect our friendship, but with my family's current financial situation, I was afraid to just let go. I looked at God, asking Him to guide me. The solution I felt in my heart was to let my friend have the money. I struggled, but then realized it was easier for me to give it to him than have him take it from me. I told him he does not owe me a cent. My prayer is that he will not need any more loans.

STRENGTH TO FORGIVE

Why would I give him the money? Why would I forgive him the debt? It was easier than making him sweat and getting myself all stressed out. I am done with all that. It was funny though, how difficult it was to let go, how hard it was to forgive a small debt of money when I had forgiven others for much deeper and more hurtful things in my life.

I suppose every decision to forgive is new in its own way, and requires some new measure of strength. A strength that only comes from God.

How many times have I gone through life without asking Him for that strength? How many times have I failed to forgive, or love, or truly live, because I did not have His power?

We live our lives, one day after the other. We breathe, in and out. So often, we constantly do the same thing. But somehow, we're expecting ... hoping ... for a different outcome. Insane, right? When that different outcome does not come, we get mad. We find an excuse. We find someone else to blame.

"I AM DONE."

That's what I often want to say. "Stick a fork in me." I am done when it feels like people blow my head off for no reason.

A relative called and offered me something, and told me to come pick it up. She knows I really like this stuff. I arranged to pick it up after work, to which she agreed. I called her as promised, and she blew me away verbally. It was obvious she was upset and I was the punching bag. She told me to come another time. My thoughts were, *I didn't call you. You called me.* It took a few minutes to shake off the words. Needless to say, I did not go pick up her goodies. I wasn't mad at her.

I am done being sad, mad, or emotionally unstable because of someone else's words. "Stick a fork in me."

My grandson is struggling with growing up and being responsible. When things do not go his way, he sometimes displays an ugly aggressiveness, or will start blaming others for not helping him out. For years, when facing this behavior, I examined myself to assure I was not being overly critical. Now I have begun to see that he will work it out eventually. I realize it is not my fault.

"I am done."

When my business is too busy and my head is filled with too much information, I schedule a date with my friend. We will get together and sew for hours. Sometimes I go to Sees Candies and purchase pecan buddies, swing by Starbucks to get a large coffee with hazelnut, and take in a movie alone. My golf clubs are in my trunk in case I find myself in a place where I want to get away. Other times I will play the food court game on my phone. If anybody has a problem with that, too bad. For your information, I'm on level 40.

There is a place for balance. We are not meant to always go, go, go. There is a time to stop and rest and rejuvenate, to decompress from everything that we tend to carry on our shoulders.

"Stick a fork in me."

Yes, I give myself away very often, and as a result, can feel weary at the giving, like I will never be whole or complete.

But there are times I run and hide myself in God. By God's grace, these times are coming more often.

I can only bless people because I am blessed. A car that never stops to refill with gas will eventually stop altogether.

God is my source, my strength. Every time I become weary, somebody does or says something that energizes me. That's God right there, using His still small voice to speak to others and bring a blessing my way.

Driving down the street one extremely cold day, I saw a lady walking down the street. Without thinking, I turned my truck around and helped her little old body up into my husband's tall truck.

Asking her where she was headed, I dropped her off at the grocer's. She explained to me she was 84 years old and needed to go shopping. As she was departing from the vehicle, she said, "Everything you have given out, you will get back." Her statement made me burst into tears thinking I don't have room for everything. How could that be?

Somebody always says or does something that causes me to want to continue this narrow road. Thank you, Lord. In Hebrew "grace is a place where one lives." Only grace can be so wonderful, so forgiving a place.

GIVING FORGIVENESS, GAINING CLOSURE:

To Jethro (a 70-year-old man)

You had no earthly business touching me. Your mind was sick. I hated you then, and told myself that I would hate you forever.

But not anymore.

I was only six years old. How dare you?

I can smell the dusty, moldy attic, the smell of insulation. Occasionally, I taste your cigar tongue in my mouth. I feel the tears of my six-year-old body as you penetrated me.

I pray with all my heart that you repented before you died. I pray that all the children you violated have found the way of escape and no longer live in the box they created to protect themselves from you. I pray your wife didn't get hurt by your violations.

I refuse to hate you.
I refuse to be bound by the violations.
I forgive you.

Chapter Two
Dragging Our Past into the Future

There is therefore now no condemnation to them which are in Christ Jesus, who walk not after the flesh, but after the Spirit. For the law of the Spirit of life in Christ Jesus hath made me free from the law of sin and death. (Romans 8:1-2)

Anytime we drag our past into future, we have some grieving to do. We have to stop and do just that; otherwise, we hang on to the weight of life's circumstances. All that extra weight slows us down and robs us of new life.

Grief is one of the most healing events in life. We fear it, but we don't have to. They say that the eyes are the windows to the soul, so in a way, those tears are washing the soul clean, so it can see and experience life in its fullest.

Reintroducing our past into our future is painful, yes, but it is also necessary. Dealing with the pain of the past allows us to be open and honest in relationships, lower our defenses, and stop being deceitful—to ourselves most of all.

FINDING FREEDOM BY RELEASING PAIN

Releasing hurts is a challenge. It means losing something we have had for years. But there is nothing like the freedom that comes from letting go of the pain. Some losses are necessary: weight, pain, old friends.

We tend to fear pain. We run from it by keeping busy. We hide from it by refusing to look back. But using the human body as a comparison, pain is a good thing. When we feel pain, we are alerted that something is wrong.

For years, people thought that leprosy attacked the body and it slowly rotted and died. But doctors and researchers finally discovered that it was not the leprosy itself. It was the lack of physical sensations that caused someone with leprosy to keep walking with a broken ankle, or keeping working with a fractured bone. The lack of pain eventually brought about a slow death.

Leprosy is not the only such illness that causes damage related to lack of feeling. Syphilis causes a mouth sore that is painless. With diabetics, the toes get numb. Any sores that diabetics contract are hard to heal because of lack of circulation. A paraplegic or quadriplegic might not feel pain, but their immobility to move anything from neck down, or from the back down, is its own kind of pain. And because they cannot feel it when they develop bedsores, they must be moved about on a regular basis, or sores can get infected and cause serious damage to their bodies.

We don't like pain, but we need it. It is part of our physiology for a purpose. When the indicators point to something being wrong, we can fix it.

If there is no pain, we ignore a problem. Emotionally, when we are running away from pain, we might try to mask it or cover it over. But this will never work over a long term. Our normal pathway changes due to hiding our true selves from the pain. Then we have to do things differently. We start to cope differently. The way we express our emotions start to change. We develop insecurity, low self-esteem. We start to isolate ourselves. We begin to show signs of physical problems such as overeating, anorexia, or even "over cleaning," just to push back the pain.

We might try to make the situation seem small, or pretend that we were not hurt by it. But what we really need to do is separate it from the whole so it can be dealt with. This involves honesty with ourselves, and often with others as well.

The biggest lie you might hear about pain and grief is that time heals all wounds. Time may change the wound, but the scar remains, constantly reminding us of the wound.

Only God heals all wounds.

And only if we let Him.

Circumstances sometimes make us bitter or hateful. We might feel rejected by those we love most. We could end up in denial to the bitterness or the grief. We need healing.

God heals wounds to a point where the scars are invisible.

Do we believe that God can truly heal all wounds? Only with belief comes healing.

Chapter Three

Splat

*But now, O Lord, thou art our father;
we are the clay, and thou our potter;
and we all are the work of thy hand. (Isaiah 64:8)*

It's the sound of wet clay hitting the Potter's wheel. Yes, He has something specific in mind. A purpose. A plan. But all we often hear is the "splat." We feel it, too. Painful and harsh.

Some people might understand this concept more easily than others. The difference will often be a person's walk with God, and their will to let God be God in their lives. God does not want to be God only of the pieces we hand over to Him, but He wants to be God over our entire existence. As our Lord and Creator, He has that right. At the same time, He is not a God who forces His way into our world. He patiently waits for us to realize He doesn't need our help to give us everything He wants us to have.

It's far easier when we choose to let Him have full sway.

I was taught this in a Women's Worship experience. The teacher said she sat on the Potter's wheel for a long time, wanting to be done with it, but God kept saying, "No." She wanted to get off the wheel because the transformation was uncomfortable, but she sensed God's answer: "No, it's not your time."

The only thing that kept her on that wheel was her. She wanted what the Potter had for her, so she made a conscious decision to stay on that wheel until God said she was ready to get off. She didn't fully understand, but she was willing to give her life over to the will of God.

She said she never regretted it.

GOD'S JOB AT THE POTTER'S WHEEL

In the Book of Romans, Paul asks an interesting question. It seems to be a rhetorical question, because there is only one possible answer. The verse states, "O man, who art thou that replies against God? Shall the thing formed say to him that formed it, 'Why have you made me thus?'"

The only obvious answer is, "No one." We are no one to reply to the Potter, who is our Creator and Redeemer, and the Author and Finisher of our faith, and ask Him, "Are you done yet? I'm tired of being on this wheel. And what are you making of me anyway? I'm not sure I like it."

That's not our place. God is the Potter. And as he sets us gently on the wheel and begins spinning, here are some things to keep in mind:

- God gives us guidance.
- He tells us what He wants from us.
- He keeps us on the wheel until He is done.
- He puts us back on the wheel at His time.
- He is right, always!
- He takes all of our cares.
- He clears our mind.

OUR JOB ON THE POTTER'S WHEEL

So while we are there, spinning away, sometimes trying our best to yield, sometimes wondering what on earth God is doing, what is our responsibility? First of all, it is not our job to question God. It is our job to trust. It is our job to have faith. We can remember that faith and trust comes through spending time with the Lord, in His Word, the Bible.

Counseling with Godly friends and acquaintances will likely benefit us as well as help us find perspective.

Here are a few things to keep in mind about our "job" on the Potter's wheel:

- We have no control.

- We are free from all the cares of our lives. In Scripture, Jesus tells us to cast all our cares upon Him, stating that He cares for us (1 Peter 5:7).
- We have a choice to stay or leave.
- We have to give Him control.
- Our mind is clear when we give Him ultimate control.

There is a story in the Bible, in the Book of Acts. Jesus had died, risen, and ascended back to Heaven. His disciples were still on earth, and they had begun to proclaim His truth and salvation to all who would listen (and to many who would not). One day, two of Jesus' disciples went up to the temple to pray, and a miracle took place. The story went like this:

> *Now Peter and John went up together into the temple at the hour of prayer, being the ninth hour. And a certain man lame from his mother's womb was carried, whom they laid daily at the gate of the temple which is called Beautiful, to ask alms of them that entered into the temple; Who seeing Peter and John about to go into the temple asked an alms.*
>
> *And Peter, fastening his eyes upon him with John, said, Look on us. And he gave heed unto them, expecting to receive something of them. Then Peter said, Silver and gold have I none; but such as I have give I thee: In the name of Jesus Christ of Nazareth rise up and walk. (Acts 3:1-6)*

Peter gave what he had. He might have thought it was little. No silver. No gold. No money. But He had the power of the risen Savior and the man was healed. Scripture tells us the man "leaping up stood, and walked, and entered with them into the temple, walking, and leaping, and praising God" (Acts 3:8).

One question we can ask every day is, "What do I have to give?" We might feel that we have nothing. No silver. No gold. Little money. Only enough for ourselves. No energy. No talents. Little, so little, to speak of.

But do we? We who have called on the name of Jesus have His power coursing through our spirits today. We can also claim His promises of healing and renewal, for ourselves and for our loved ones. For our past, our present, and our future.

We can rise up and walk. We can leap and praise God.

We can be a testimony of God's unlimited healing power.

What do I have?

With God, everything!

GIVING FORGIVENESS, GAINING CLOSURE:

To Joe

All I wanted was to be loved as was appropriate.

I realized that you did love me, but inappropriately. When I confronted you at the age of 86, when I told you my pain at the way you had treated me, you asked me for sex again.

I was done. I knew the healing was not going to come from your apology. Even at age 93, you still asked me for sex. It didn't hurt anymore, though, because I had already forgiven you.

I forgave you when we prayed together, you asked for forgiveness, and you asked me for sex again and again.

I purposefully brought you raisin cookies, pound cake, and bananas. With these gifts, I was stepping over the boundaries I had built for myself. I purposefully got in your face and learned to love you despite your rotten heart.

I forgave you when you needed help putting on that shirt. Touching your body to help you just because you needed it changed my heart.

I watched you in the hospital violate those nurses and your family laughed, thinking it was funny while I almost puked.

I was there when you were taking your final breaths, hoping God was whispering in your ear to repent.

I know I am only one of the many you violated and pray God please help them love themselves. Help them know this man is sick and they were not the cause of these actions. I wanted to hate you and I had valid reasons to hate. But I will not spend that energy hating.

I will instead expend my energy telling others how mercy does endure, how forgiveness is freedom, and that God is love.

I survived.

Chapter Four
Prayer Changes Things

The Lord is nigh unto all them that call upon him, to all that call upon him in truth. He will fulfil the desire of them that fear him: he also will hear their cry, and will save them. (Psalm 145:18-19)

Sometimes, when we're on the Potter's wheel, we feel there is nothing we can do but wait. But there is always something we can do.

Prayer is a powerful statement of faith in our Heavenly Father. It is also our mode of connection with Him. It is through prayer that we draw near to God, and realize that as we do so, He draws near to us. It is also through prayer that we bring our requests before Him, and discover just how powerful and wise He is.

The Apostle Paul urged the early Christians with these words: "Be careful for nothing; but in everything by prayer and supplication with thanksgiving let your requests be made known unto God" (Philippians 4:5-7). It tells us that nothing is too big or too small to bring before the throne of grace. It also tells us that giving thanks to God is a key element in prayer.

In another book of the Bible, this time to the Romans, Paul said, "Likewise the Spirit also helpeth our infirmities: for we know not what we should pray for as we ought: but the Spirit itself maketh intercession for us with groanings which cannot be uttered" (Romans 8:25-27).

This is a beautiful promise, because there are times we feel we cannot pray. The heart is too heavy. The mind is too confused. The soul feels empty. But at these times, the Holy Spirit will pray through us, and we need not fear that we are too weak to pray.

Prayer is so powerful that we are asked in scripture to, "Pray without ceasing" (1 Thess. 5:17). This does not mean that at every moment we must be on our hands and knees in prayer, but more that, whatever we are doing, we can turn our minds and spirits toward our heavenly Father, and know that He is near and ready to answer.

EXPECT A CHANGE

Our own expectations and faith are an important aspect in receiving answers to prayer. So often, we tend to think our prayers are not answered, when the answers to our questions are already in God's Word. We read statements like, "Ye ask, and receive not, because ye ask amiss, that ye may consume it upon your lusts" (James 4:3). Our prayers are powerful, but we must first align our will with God's in order to find the answer to prayer.

Timing is also important. Perhaps God's answer is yes, but also, wait. There are men and women of God who prayed every day for years for the same thing, or the same person. But there are many other things at play that we cannot see. Above all, we must understand that God has a perfect will. In His time, He will bring it to pass.

THE GREAT SUPPER

Sometimes, when we pray, we might feel far from the presence of God. Other times, we feel almost that we can reach out and touch the gates of Heaven. Obviously, in one of these examples, it is easy to pray. In the other, it might feel impossible.

We might feel so far away from the presence of God, but we can know that we are all invited. We are invited to enter into His presence at any time through prayer. We are invited to His banquet, where all can find food for the soul.

Jesus told a parable about a banquet with unexpected guests:

> *Then said he unto him, A certain man made a great supper, and bade many: And sent his servant at supper time to say to them that were bidden, Come; for all things are now ready.*

> *And they all with one consent began to make excuse. The first said unto him, I have bought a piece of ground, and I must needs go and see it: I pray thee have me excused.*
>
> *And another said, I have bought five yoke of oxen, and I go to prove them: I pray thee have me excused.*
>
> *And another said, I have married a wife, and therefore I cannot come.*
>
> *So that servant came, and shewed his lord these things. Then the master of the house being angry said to his servant, Go out quickly into the streets and lanes of the city, and bring in hither the poor, and the maimed, and the halt, and the blind.*
>
> *And the servant said, Lord, it is done as thou hast commanded, and yet there is room.*
>
> *And the lord said unto the servant, Go out into the highways and hedges, and compel them to come in, that my house may be filled.*
>
> *For I say unto you, That none of those men which were bidden shall taste of my supper.*
> *(Luke 14: 16-24)*

In this scripture, a Master is inviting all the "chosen people" to his banquet. Although the Master feels his banquet is a big event, these chosen people don't. They have concerns of their own and choose not to attend this event. This is an example of the invitation we have to come into the

Kingdom of God. To feast on God's provision given us, all we have to do is come. But this particular invite was given to God's chosen people in the Old Testament.

The Master's servant invited many, but they all had excuses. Just married. Bought some oxen and had to try them out. Bought some land and had to go see it. They blew off the invitation to this grand event. The Master was appalled.

Who were the servants inviting the chosen to this great banquet? They were the prophets in the Old Testament. God used them in many ways to convince the Jews to come to Him. They were not chosen because of anything they had done, and God promised them they would be as many as the stars in the sky or sand by the seashore. God delivered them many times and there remained the truth they rejected Him yet again.

When the servant reported to His Master with the message that the elite refused His invitation, the Master replied, "Go get the poor, disfigured, crippled, and the blind. How blessed you will be that they have nothing to pay you. You will be repaid at the resurrection of the righteous."

After the elite refused the banquet, the Master invited all who would not refuse Him. We, as Gentiles, are now invited to partake in the Grand Banquet with God through Jesus.

Though circumstances have caused our road to be harder, different, and painful, though we are part of the maimed—the cripple that waited at the pool for 38 years, or the woman who suffered with issues for 12 years—the fact remains that we are invited to the Grand Banquet with Christ.

THE BANQUET AND US

What does that Grand Banquet mean to us? What Banquet has the power to enable us to take steps forward, away from the past? What Banquet lets us live free from the hurt, pain, and dysfunction that Satan used through the person that abused us?

The Banquet, for us, means that Jesus Himself through the Holy Spirit intercedes for us to God through groans only He understands. He knows about the road we had to take to get here, and He ever lives to make intercession for us (Hebrews 7:25). Jesus prays for us.

Satan's job is to make sure we fail by accusing us to God. He goes back and forth accusing the brethren to God. He would have us live in shame, but God through Christ's resurrection delivered us out of the shame. Satan accuses us and reminds us that what happened to us was wrong, and he blames us. But God, through Christ, said the person who violated us was wrong, and if we violated others, that was wrong. In spite of it all, we are new creatures through repentance and salvation. Old things are passed away and all things are made new.

Our mind is new, thoughts are new, actions are new, and our heart is new. From the day we were invited to the Banquet to this day, we can feast on the goodness of salvation.

OLD THINGS ARE PASSED AWAY

When bird eggs hatch, the mama bird feeds the baby with her mouth. It is the same as human infants who depend on their mother to feed them. But there comes a time when the baby grows up and needs to start making decisions for himself or herself.

We are no different, spiritually speaking. God has allowed us choices. We have the freedom to decide for ourselves. We have to decide if the choices we make are working for our good. We can't, at the age of 12 years, receive milk by suckling at our mothers. Our life-sustaining nourishment comes from God Himself, through the redemption blood of Christ.

How does this work for us? Before we make decisions, we need to ask ourselves:

- How would this decision affect my being right before God?

- Would God be pleased with this decision?
- How can I fix this if I messed up?

When making decisions, some of the most important things to remember are:

- It doesn't matter what other people think about me. Only God's perspective matters.
- Check the Word of God for truth. Truth is not a matter of how I feel; it is a matter of what God says.
- I need to forgive myself quickly, repent when I mess up, and get back on the path quickly.
- It is not my place to seek different opinions about things; I must check the Word. If I receive differing opinions, the right opinion is found in the Word of God.
- I am not perfect, but God is. In this knowledge, I can give myself a break.
- In order reach the mark, I have to know what the mark is. The mark is to please God with the life I chose. The mark is the high calling of God.
- Most of all, the prize is not given to the swift or the strong but the one who finishes the race.

About this "race of life," Paul said, "Let us lay aside every weight, and the sin which doth so easily beset us, and let us run with patience the race that is set before us" (Hebrews 12:1b).

Who in their right mind would carry weights to run a race? Weights are burdensome when trying to move fast, or going for the long haul. Patience is hard to find when you are burdened. Let go of those weights. Put them down. And run the race of life, no matter what the course looks like.

How can we find strength to do this?

"...Looking unto Jesus, the Author and Finisher of our faith" (Hebrews 12:2a).

Chapter Five
Big-Girl Moves

I have learned to be content regardless of circumstances. I know what it is to be in want, and I know what it is to have more than enough — in everything and in every way I have learned the secret of being full and being hungry, of having abundance and being in need. I can do all things through him who gives me power. (Phil. 4:11b-13)

That's the secret: find the path to the Father in the midst of circumstance. This can be difficult for most, but not impossible. If God is God in the good times, He is the same God in the bad times. The difference is our focus. We need to focus on God and not the problem.

We cannot change every situation, nor is every situation caused by us. When Mama passed away, God was God. When members of my family were raped, God was God. Was it easy? No, but the situations were livable as opposed to me wanting to lie down and die.

"What, then, are we to say to these things? If God is for us, who can be against us?" (Romans 8: 31). Can we believe that? Yes, with all our hearts, because God is for us. He sent His Son to die for our sins and to reunite us with the Father. There is no love like that.

We proclaim in our hearts and minds whether we believe God or not. If we believe God is for us, whom shall we fear? Our problems and situations often appear so large. They deeply affect our lives, but if God is with us, He is with us. God often causes us to change, not the problem. When we change our hearts, we can think clearer. When we are quiet, we can hear God's guidance.

The young prophet Jeremiah prayed with wonder in his heart, "You made heaven and earth by your great power and outstretched arm; nothing is too hard for you" (Jeremiah 32:17). God has already given us His power to complete any task set before us. We have already proclaimed God is for us, therefore we should fear no one.

Believe and proclaim with everything that is in you, "God is God in every situation and circumstance."

We should ask ourselves, "What is too hard for Him?" Then we should answer with resounding affirmation, "Nothing!"

"God, your way is holiness. What god is as great as God?" (Psalms 77:13). Again, the answer is clear. Only God is God. The one true God.

NOT A GARBAGE CAN

Peace I leave with you, my peace I give unto you: not as the world giveth, give I unto you. Let not your heart be troubled, neither let it be afraid. (John 14:27)

When we are given a gift, the only way we can lose that particular gift is to give it away. Peace is given us now through Christ. Let us make sure we keep that gift.

We acquire the skill of preserving our peace with practice. In the midst of conversations, we decide whether or not this is necessary information for our lives. We can ask questions like, "Is this information going to benefit my spirit and cause it to grow?"

If not, the person conversing should be informed to take that trash elsewhere. We could let them finish and ignore the information, but that behavior reinforces people to bring more trash.

Determine that you are not a garbage can. Your objective is to redirect verbal garbage to be taken elsewhere. This redirecting can and should be done in a manner so that God would be pleased. We must remember in all our relationships that God resists the proud, but gives grace to the humble (James 4:6).

Chapter Six
Measure It Up

Jesus said unto them, 'Because of your unbelief: for verily I say unto you, If ye have faith as a grain of mustard seed, ye shall say unto this mountain, Remove hence to yonder place; and it shall remove; and nothing shall be impossible unto you. Howbeit this kind goeth not out but by prayer and fasting.' (Matthew 17: 20-21)

"*N*othing shall be impossible to you" means nothing. *No* thing. Jesus made this statement. This statement informs me that if Jesus is in me, I can do all things. Most of all, I can live free.

BIGGER THAN GOD?
Things and stuff are not bigger than God. What can I compare to Him? My faith, Jesus said, has to as big as a head of a stickpin. A small seed. Mustard seeds grow into large plants in some climates, but they start out the size of a pencil tip. Jesus choose a mustard seed in this parable, saying that faith of that miniscule size is enough to move mountains.

Usually the mountain that needs to be moved is me. Situations and circumstances occur, sometimes cast upon us by someone else. But the culprit of the circumstance goes forward, and we get stuck. We get stuck in not being able to forgive ourselves for mistakes, or not being able to forgive people who said or did something against us. We look at ourselves, missing what God sees. We get so busy criticizing and judging ourselves that we fail to get a glimpse of His forgiveness. Loving ourselves is out of the question.

Others evaluate us and render their comments and we wear those comments like clothes. Daily, as we dress, we are sure to bring the comments, evaluations, and judgment of others. What would it take to stop the madness? Measure it up.

Take an imaginary measuring tape. Ask yourself, "How many inches will it take on each side to make this situation work in my favor? How much time or space on each side and the circumstance is complete? Who is in the picture that does not benefit my goals and vision?"

An older woman once said, "If a person is not with you, he's against you." Who's in your circle who is willing to work put forth effort on your behalf?

MOVING FORWARD

Once, as a nurse, I went to a client's home to treat a gunshot wound. The client was a young beautiful woman who had been shot in the arm. Her bone was shattered and she had pins and screws holding her bone in place to heal properly.

The young woman informed me that her "boyfriend shot her." How come that same young man was lying beside her? My brain doesn't compute that my friend would cause harm to me, or even cause me to be in a harmful environment. Someone who causes harm to me is not my friend. Someone who causes harm to you is not your BFF. Please don't get stuck in unfriendly relationships.

What will it take to move forward? Do you have mustard seed faith?

God has not called us to the spirit of fear, but of power, love, and a sound mind (2 Timothy 1:7). Maintaining unhealthy relationships are usually done because we fear being alone, or we fear not being accepted. We fear living outside the box of cliques.

God created people with a longing to be loved. It is not unusual be want to be loved, but at what cost? That is the question we must answer honestly. Love is free, and maintaining an unhealthy relationship is not of a sound mind. When people criticize us daily to keep our esteem low, it is unhealthy.

I believe that some people grow up in an environment in which they had no examples of real love. At some point, however, we must stand up for ourselves and inform our culprits that this type of affection is not what we desire in this relationship. If people cannot receive it after being given an opportunity to change the behavior that inflicting pain, that is the true reflection of what they feel about you. Have courage to move away from such relationships.

Habits are hard to break. It may take time to redirect behavior from negative to positive, but it is well worth the effort. When our true friends love us, they will do what it takes because their desire is not to hurt us. On the other hand, if a person refuses to change those behaviors and does not care about your emotions or needs, that person is probably not right for you.

Spend some time and determine who is in your circle. Take out the measuring tape and ask the Lord for a mustard seed of faith. Then measure twice, with prayer and love, and cut away.

GIVING FORGIVENESS, GAINING CLOSURE:

To Otis (a 34-year-old man)

After your violation, I in turn violated someone else. Lord, I am so very sorry. B, I am so very sorry. I pray my apology to you helped you. I wish you would have let me show you more, but I understand.

Lord, please release her from the pain I caused. Please cause her heart to be free to love and live. Release freedom from bondage in her mind for her children and their children.

Bestow Your love on her and her entire family and cause her to forgive those who come against her. Her father will not have the power over me any longer. I forgive him with every fiber of my being this day.

Chapter Seven
Perception of a Situation

For as he thinketh in his heart, so is he.
(Proverbs 23:7)

Our perception of any given situation is a combination of a few things. It takes into account our intelligence and knowledge, along with how a situation appears to us. In other words, perception is subjective. The things we see —appearance and visions—are perceived in ways that depend on the state of our heart and mind. Perception is our take on what we hear and see. Our perception is not always correct because of the way we "see" things in our minds.

When we have been betrayed, abused, and lied to so very often, it is easier to believe a lie than the truth. When a person doesn't keep a promise, or rolls their eyes, or doesn't speak to us as usual, we take that personally. Because of our personal history, we usually perceive it as rejection.

Rejection can cause us great discomfort, even if sometimes the person is not rejecting us purposely. Cold shoulders are hurtful and magnified in our perception. Why? Because we are victims and the hurtful experiences we have faced in life has caused our thought process to be filtered through the perception that we will always be victims. Because of this, we are re-victimized repeatedly ... in our minds.

Many situations and circumstances are not even about us, but we fit our victim mentality into the situation so we can have a reason to be hurt, as usual. Our perceptions create self-fulfilling prophecies in which we are hurt again and again.

AS A MAN THINKS

Scripture tells us, "As a man thinketh in his heart, so is he" (Proverbs 23:7). What we need to do is let go of our limited and warped self-perception and take on the mind of Christ. We need to realize that we are wonderfully made in the image and likeness of God. In the beginning, God said, "Let's create mankind in our image and likeness," and so He did.

That's me: a beautiful spirit of God in a human body. I am an heir of God. His inheritance is mine. Why would I walk around looking poor, acting poor, being without hope and help if I am the spirit of God, and created in His image?

God has never failed me yet, and I hope my faith is at least as big as a mustard seed. Big situations and circumstances will not make me think I am anything less than what He has created me to be.

Tell yourself today, "I am fearfully and wonderfully made. I am made in the image of God. I am treasured by God and no one can change the love that God has for me. I will walk in newness of life."

MAKING UP STORIES

Our imagination often makes up stories to justify our feelings. This is because we don't take the time to investigate the rest of the story. If that person doesn't call you back, it doesn't mean that they are avoiding you. They may have been in a car accident and died. I know that's far-fetched, and hopefully nothing that drastic ever happens. But it could be true that they just forgot. And if it is true, is it possible to forgive them?

You might have been overlooked on the list. Perhaps this is why they invited you to a party at the last minute or not at all. These things do happen, but they do not define who you are.

I truly believe people are not in some room somewhere contemplating how to make me feel like I don't belong. Conclusions like that only make me feel less than worthy, undervalued, and unappreciated. And that is not who God says I am.

It is not who God says you are either.

DON'T JUMP TO CONCLUSIONS

Judge not, that ye be not judged. For with what judgment ye judge, ye shall be judged: and with what measure ye mete, it shall be measured to you again. (Matthew 7:1-2).

Those are sobering words, for each one of us has at some point in time judged without due reason. When you find yourself judging a situation or a person without knowing the full picture, listen for the rest of the story. Everyone deserves the courtesy not to be accused or judged. We would like the same treatment from others, and the "Golden Rule" calls us to this. Remember: "Do unto others as you would have them do unto you" (Luke 6:31).

Because of our mentality, we often expect the worst first, but what if this is not the case? Is it possible that this story has a happy ending, and no one means to harm us?

It will take a rewiring of your thought process to allow yourself this happy ending. No conclusions should be made until the end of the story. You probably don't like to hear about the ending of a riveting movie before you watch it, or a great book before you read it. Allow yourself to be pleasantly surprised in your life as well. The Lord is the "Author" and "Finisher" of our lives. And something tells me that what He has in mind is greater than anything we could ask or think.

THAT ONE DOESN'T COUNT

Often, the things we take the wrong way, or perceive as rejection, are simple misunderstandings. Well, guess what? Communication is simple. We often tend to think it's difficult, time consuming, or not worth the trouble. But there are things we can do to help create positive communication with those in our life. Yes, it may be difficult, but it's not impossible.

Communication goes two ways. If I have a problem with someone, I have a few options. I need to 1) tell them, 2) resolve it, or 3) move on.

Likewise, if someone has a problem with me, they need to tell me. If they choose not to tell me, it doesn't count. I can't address an issue if I don't know what it is. We tend to realize there is an issue when we see the rolling eyes, feel the avoidance or rejection, and hear the second-hand gossip.

Even so, we have choices. One choice could be to confront them (but if so, we had better be ready for the response). Hurtful gestures are just that: "hurtful." People who display such behavior are hurt. Offend in Hebrew means "bad wind." Wind in Hebrew means "spirit." Bad spirit is intentional.

Often we do and say stupid stuff unintentionally offending. These instances can be resolved with simple communication.

When I review in my heart what could have been the issue, I often choose to call or confront people with an honest, heart-filled apology. My intent is not to hurt anyone. For others, I have given a "generic" apology, heart-felt but generic because I don't know what I have done to cause them to have an issue with me.

Even with both of these scenarios, the story doesn't always end with the desired result. Don't get upset. Think on the things of God. Was your apology honest with the person, with yourself, and with God? If so move on, and love that person anyway. Move on.

Don't be Pressured in Conversations

Have you ever been in a conversation where you knew from the beginning that you were being pressured into something? If so, it's likely true that when that person made the decision to call or visit you, their objective was to pressure you. They may not have said it to themselves in that manner, but they had a goal in mind for calling you. Their points were so valid and you were left with all the responsibility on your shoulders.

There have been times I have made phone calls when I really wanted the end of that conversation to be in my favor. I have only realized afterward that those times have been moments when I failed to turn the situation over to the Lord and tell Him, "Not my will, but thine be done." It is at times when we think we have to control a situation and work it out that we tend to get uptight, upset, and more forceful than necessary.

Whether you are on the giving end or receiving end of this type of conversation, trust is a key factor. Trust that God has everything under control.

Clear communication erases confusion. Take time to review the conversation in your mind, and don't make decisions abruptly. Pray. Ask God first. The exchange of a few words can move mountains. Don't take on tasks that will push you over the cliff of busyness to insane.

Ask God if you are to help, where you are to help, and how much you should or should not help. Rendering help "just because someone asked," and rendering it with an attitude doesn't count before God.

Chapter Eight
When I Get Stuck

For I am persuaded, that neither death, nor life, nor angels, nor principalities, nor powers, nor things present, nor things to come, Nor height, nor depth, nor any other creature, shall be able to separate us from the love of God, which is in Christ Jesus our Lord. (Romans 8:38-39)

Because I am having a human experience in this spiritual body, I sometimes make mistakes. In the past, mistakes would hold me back from any kind of progress for weeks at a time. Every day, I would wake up repenting for that mistake. I would get stuck and apologize to God, yet still feel unable to move forward in my spiritual life.

Today, I am fully persuaded that nothing—not death, life, angels, devils, height, or depth—can separate me from the Love of God that is in Christ. Talking to myself, I say, "Move on. Okay, it happened. Put one foot in front of the other and get going forward."

Lessons are learned from mistakes and mistakes remind me to go to God first before I make decisions.

KEEP YOUR MIND

> *Finally, brethren, whatsoever things are true, whatsoever things are honest, whatsoever things are just, whatsoever things are pure, whatsoever things are lovely, whatsoever things are of good report; if there be any virtue, and if there be any praise, think on these things. (Phil. 4:8)*

World news reports this. Local news reports that. With job and family, there is enough to keep your mind busy. One thing we all forget is that God is in the midst of it all. The president would not be elected unless God allows. God allows earthquakes and floods from the cursed ground and will until the earth is redeemed with His people. Our loved ones come and they go because God says so. All these things and more happens because God is the Creator of all things.

Often my mind wonders and worries about so many things I have absolutely no control over. I also tend to worry about some things I do have control over, such as money and bills. It is during those times that more and more often, I'm learning to ask God for help with my decision-making. When I ask for help, the results of the matter is beyond what I asked for.

In two years' time, my husband and I have decreased our debt from $200,000 to less than $15,000. Today, I try to stay before God with issues because I have found that He not only resolves those He is concerned with, but He also resolves them above and beyond what I ask or even think.

PERFECT PEACE

Thou wilt keep him in perfect peace, whose mind is stayed on thee: because he trusteth in thee.
(Isaiah 26:3)

The secret is my mind is stayed on Him. Some situations are disturbing and depressing. Depression is normal in some circumstances—for short periods but not prolonged periods. For example: If your child is sent to jail, or murdered, or a loved one passes away, grief is a normal and natural result.

The difference with believers is that we believe God for everything, not as the world believes, but as children of God. As children of God, we focus on God. He is a healer and consoler. We can say with confidence, "What is impossible for Him?"

This is where the rubber meets the road, and we put up or shut up. Either God is God of everything and I give this to Him, with thanks and praises, or He is the God of nothing and I can't allow Him to keep me in this time of trouble. For most of us, this progress toward perfect peace is a process and takes time. Just remember, time does not heal all wounds, but God does.

MY PEACE

Peace I leave with you, my peace I give unto you: not as the world giveth, give I unto you. Let not your heart be troubled, neither let it be afraid. (John 14:27)

"My peace I give freely," Christ spoke in the Gospel of John. If it were a human saying, "I give you my peace," you might want to run for the hills. But when Christ says something, it will not come back void. He can't lie as God's Son, because God can't lie.

We can honestly "let not our heart be troubled." We can truly "neither be afraid." What can we be so assured about? EVERYTHING. No thing is too hard for Him. Problems shrink under God. Some things are so out of our hands, it doesn't matter how much we worry; we can't change it anyway.

If you find yourself worrying and fretting, slow down. Don't allow yourself to do things in the same old manner. We are new creatures. Think on things that are pure and of good report. Don't be afraid; be new.

TEST THE SPIRIT FOR TRUTH

Beloved, believe not every spirit, but try the spirits whether they are of God: because many false prophets are gone out into the world. Hereby know ye the Spirit of God: Every spirit that confesseth that Jesus Christ is come in the flesh is of God: And every spirit that confesseth not that Jesus Christ is come in the flesh is not of God: and this is that spirit of antichrist, whereof ye have heard that it should come; and even now already is it in the world. (1 John 4:1-3)

Why, someone might ask, is this important? This is important because we should not be involved in matters that don't concern us.

If Cousin Mooky and others are fighting over who bought the beer and who is drinking too much of it, this doesn't concern us. If someone knows you are saved and starts a purposeful argument about their god compared to your God, this doesn't concern you. Don't argue back.

A good friend said to me long ago, "He saw a fool fighting, but he couldn't tell which one was the fool." This means that there were two people fighting. Someone looking in from the outside couldn't tell which one was the fool. Don't be the fool; stay out of senseless arguments.

If you are hanging around people or places where the spirit of the world is rampant, you will find ungodly attitudes clinging to you. The enemy of your soul will try to convince you that it is okay to fill yourself with stuff that is purposefully against the spirit of God. That is so not cool. Evil communication does corrupt good manners, and this can include communication with certain family members.

Chapter Nine
Oscars vs. Piranhas

Behold, I send you forth as sheep in the midst of wolves: be ye therefore wise as serpents, and harmless as doves. (Matthew 10:16)

In the Bible, Genesis notes that the serpent was slick. We know that of Satan, but note the behavior of these fish: the Oscar and piranha.

Piranhas only travels in schools or with their cliques. They do this so that they won't be caught alone, making them vulnerable to predators. Their teeth are their weapons—sharp as knives. They use them to puncture and shear their prey.

When piranha smell blood, they perceive weakness. Their manner of attack is to circle their prey so fast that in a matter of seconds, their prey no longer exists. In 1913, Theodore Roosevelt went to the Amazon where the local fishermen proved a point. The fishermen blocked a part of the river for two days where the piranha lived. After two days, they dropped a cow in the water, and within a few seconds, there was no proof of the cow. That disturbing event prompted Theodore Roosevelt to write a book about the Amazon rainforest.

Why is this important? There were times I found myself in relationships with piranha-type friends who attempted (and sometimes succeeded) in taking everything from me, leaving me invisible. Needless to say, I remembered my Father, who has slaves treated better than that. I went back home, where my Father welcomed me and threw a party. It is not only prodigal sons who are welcomed by the heavenly Father. He watches for prodigal daughters too.

THE OSCARS

But the end of all things is at hand: be ye therefore sober, and watch unto prayer. (1 Peter 4:7)

Oscars are fish who are fed other fish. Most people purchase carp as feeder fish for the oscar. The oscar is slick. I have never seen an oscar eat, but the evidence was always there. Half a fish floating in the water or none left ... except the oscar. He is slow swimming and can grow huge if placed in a large environment. The oscar works alone. He doesn't need to be a clique.

This fish represents a person who is patient and appears kind, but is ugly inside. There is no evidence during the dating period that he is a predator ... until you wake up headless. If you look at the oscar, even when you see a fish with its head missing, there is no evidence the oscar did it. He continues to swim slowly, looking innocent. This one is not your BFF (note to self).

I believe people with these behaviors are sad on the inside. They receive "pleasure" making others sad, but whatever pleasure they might gain is fleeting and empty. They know the look of the vulnerable and are on a constant lookout for prey.

We must test the spirit of those we hang out with, to see if it agrees with the Spirit of God in us. We must always be prayerful, sober, and vigilant. God desires to hedge us about with His protection, but we must also make the choices that would not put us directly in harm's way. God's Word calls us to be harmless as doves, yes, but also wise as serpents (Matthew 10:16).

GIVING FORGIVENESS, GAINING CLOSURE:

To Clarence (a 15-year-old boy)

You always scared me after that incident.
I'm not scared anymore.

I don't hate you, but I don't love you either. I forgave you a long time ago, but you died before I could tell you. I wanted you to forgive yourself and repent, but you died.

I still remember the pain as an eight-year-old girl when you raped me. I hated you for so long. When I saw you in the public, my heart raced with fear and intimidation even when I was 30.

Today, I breathe freely and daily. I survived.

I pray all the others you violated recover fully, in Jesus' Name.

Release them, you ugly, ignorant nothing. They are not yours. All who call on the Name of Christ belong to Him.

Chapter Ten
Blessed Assurance

For our conversion is in heaven from whence also we look for our Savior, the Lord Jesus Christ.
(Phil. 3:20)

Every Christian desires to have assurance of salvation, meaning the certainty of eternal life in heaven when we die or Christ returns. Many Christians, however, are unsure of whether such security exists. Is it really "once in, forever in" the moment we trust in Christ as Lord and Savior? Emphatically, yes!

A SAVING RELATIONSHIP

Following are seven ways to know we are in a saving relationship with God. If we are sure of this, we have no reason to doubt our eternal place in the presence of our heavenly Father and His Son, Jesus Christ.

1. **We have assurance of eternal life if we believe on the Name of the Son of God.**

    Who is he that overcometh the world but he that believeth that Jesus is the Son of God? (1 John 5:5)

The faith that overcomes the world allows us to see eternal life as a reality. With this perspective on life, we experience the power of God, and we love Christ with all our heart. This relationship with the Savior enables us to overcome sinful lust and selfish materialism.

2. **We have assurance of eternal life if we are honoring Christ as Lord of our lives by seeking to keep His commandments.**

And being made perfect, he became the author of eternal salvation unto all that obey Him.
(Hebrew 5:9)

3. **We have assurance of eternal life if we love the father and the Son rather than the world, and if we can overcome the influence of the world.**

Love not the world, neither the things of the world. If any man love the world the love of the Father is not in him.
(1 John 2:15)

Do you know Him?

4. **We have assurance of eternal life if we habitually and persistently practice righteousness instead of sin.**

If we know that he is righteous, we know everyone that is born of him doeth righteous.
(1 John 2:29)

Blessed Assurance

He that committed sin is of the devil.
(1 John 3:8)

These things I have written unto you that believe on the Name of the Son of God; that you may know that ye have eternal life, and that ye may believe on the Name of the Son of God.
(1 John 5:13)

5. **We have assurance of eternal life when we love the brethren.**

We know that we have passed from death to life because we love the brethren, and hereby we know that we are of the truth and shall assure our hearts before Him.
(1 John 3:14). (See also 1 John 3:19, 2:9-11).

6. **We have assurance of eternal life when we are conscious of the Holy Spirit dwelling within us.**

And hereby we know that He (Jesus Christ) abideth in us, by the Spirit He hath given us.
(1 John 3:24). (See also 1 John 4:13).

7. **We are assured of eternal life if we are endeavoring to follow the example of Jesus and live as He lived.**

He that saith He abideth in him ought himself also so to walk even as He walked.
(1 John 2:6). (See also 1 John 8:12, 13:15).

Chapter Eleven
Are you the One or Shall I look for Another?

*H*ave you ever started reading a magazine from the middle, or looked at the table of contents and only read the chapters that interested you? That's what I'm doing here: starting in the middle and going forward to the beginning.

In church one Sunday, the pastor was teaching about prayer and getting closer to God, and Him closer to us. The Spirit of the Lord came over me and the Lord reminded me of the scripture found in Matthew 11:

And it came to pass, when Jesus had made an end of commanding his twelve disciples, he departed thence to teach and to preach in their cities.

Now when John had heard in the prison the works of Christ, he sent two of his disciples, and said unto him, "Art thou he that should come, or do we look for another?"

Jesus answered and said unto them, "Go and shew John again those things which ye do hear and see: The blind receive their sight, and the lame walk, the lepers are cleansed, and the deaf hear, the dead are raised up, and the poor have the gospel preached to them." (Matthew 11:1-5)

I remembered back to when I was facing the facts. The facts are that a 70-year-old man raped me repeatedly when I was only six years old. The facts are that I can still taste his cigar tongue in my mouth, and feel the horror of him penetrating me. The facts are that three other men did this to me by the time I was 14 years old.

Those are the facts.

But in church that day, all I could do was thank God. I couldn't stop saying, "Thank you, God. Thank you, Lord." The more I said thank you, the more I was reminded of things He had done. So more "Thank you, Lord's" came.

Tears started rolling like a river. I remembered more and more the things He had done. Tears were pouring down my face and I couldn't stop thanking Him. The lady next to me starting rubbing me on my back, patting and consoling me because I was bawling like a baby. I was grateful. So very grateful for the things He had done for me.

Satan would have me be sad, but I am so grateful. I'll tell you why.

There was a day I looked at the facts closely, and I looked at God. I told God I didn't know how to do this, and if He was God, right now would be a good time to prove it. I said, "God, either you are God, or you are not." I was reminded of the scripture when John the Baptist, the cousin of Jesus, was imprisoned and he sent a few of his followers to Jesus to ask a question: "Are you the One who was meant to come, or shall I go look for another?"

I told God, point blank, this is where the rubber meets the road. I will put up or shut up. I will live or die.

One of the main components taken from me as a child was the ability to love freely. Because of fearful experiences that happened to the deepest, most personal parts of me, my love had all kinds of borders on it. "Only if you love me appropriately will I give to you what you desire."

I only realized far later that was *bondage.*

Another component was that I needed people's approval to function. I needed to have friends' approval. Cliques, groups, Twitter, Facebook. It was important for me to fit in.

That's bondage.

I was scared of my own shadow. Fears consumed me. Fear of failure. Fear of disapproval. Fear of moving forward. Fear of stepping outside my comfort zone, falling off my saddle if someone looked at me crooked, stumbling over my own feet, negative talk about myself – everything was a problem. I was the biggest problem of all.

Bondage.

Hating myself. Dreading the next day. Longing for death. Not being good enough for anything. Sick and tired of being sick and tired. Dressing up and smiling and when somebody ask how I'm doing, answering, "Good" or "Blessed of the Lord." Feeling anything but blessed.

Bondage.

I cry for that six-year-old girl, but she doesn't live here anymore. I'm not going to frost this mud pie and tell anyone that it is cherries with whipped cream. It took hard work to get to this point ... and hard work to stay here. It's easy to fall back into old habits that are not healthy. But I refuse to be in bondage any longer.

I choose to be a conqueror. In fact, I am more than a conqueror.

Nay, in all these things we are more than conquerors through him that loved us.
(Romans 8:37)

I can do all things through Christ which strengtheneth me.
(Phil 4:13)

And we know that all things work together for good to them that love God, to them who are the called according to his purpose.
(Romans 8:28)

God will take what you have, right where you are and make you huge in Him. And Him huge in you.

Those men were possessed by an evil spirit, not of God the Almighty, to do such a thing to an innocent one. But God took that very thing and used it. He uses me to help people like you to show you that you are already an overcomer because of His shelter from the storm.

They no longer have any power over you. The box we lived in for so long no longer has to surround us. The prison they set up for us to die in no longer exists. The boundaries no longer exist. Break free, because you can in the Name of Christ.

No more bondage!

KEEPING IT 100%
WHAT IT LOOKS LIKE TO BE 100%

Approach every situation every day with the mind that matches the heart of God. One may ask what does that mean? It means if someone asks you to do something you really do not want to do, say no. Don't say yes to be a people pleaser.

Keeping it 100% means not being in a group of people criticizing another and praising the Lord in another group. It means getting up and walking away from situations and people not conducive to the spirit that tells you when things are wrong.

100% can also include not being upset with your loved one even though in a court of law you will win your case, and showing 100% love toward that person.

To approach a situation 100%, smashing it with confidence and turning right around, crying because someone said you are ugly and fat. (Elijah and the Baal worshipers and Jezebel Kings 18) The truth is people have the right to their opinion, as do I. That's their opinion and there are no laws saying we have to agree. Simply disagree. Someone I love dearly said "only pick up an offence if you want it."

Truly, I understand how one would think this would not include close friends and relatives. Quite the contrary—they can be your biggest culprits, including children.

When we don't consider all we have in us before making decisions big or small, we may appear bipolar. I am a firm business person, but a gentle grandmother. My eldest grandson was doing a job for me and became offended by the fact I wanted the job completed per my standard (as a business person). Was I operating bipolar? Should I have lowered my standard and settled for a mediocre result and pay another person to finish? No, two things happened: 1) My eldest grandson finished the job and was upset with me and 2) I don't ask him to do work for me any longer.

As a grandmother, I am loving, gentle, truthful and consistent. I believe in discipline and extreme kissing with hugs; every one of my grandchildren thinks he or she is are the favorite. My eldest grandson thought I was invaded by the body snatchers.

Proverbs is rich in wisdom noting it (wisdom) is a treasure to store up, acquire it, like choice silver, guard it. Wisdom causes length to your days (3:16), give life to your spirit, and grace to your throat (words). Be disciplined in it, walk in understanding. Wisdom builds up her house and invited all to come saying "give up your simpleness"(9: 1-6).

Proverbs says "for a beautiful woman to act without wisdom (deprived of the ability to consider situations and understand) is like unto putting a gold ring on the snout of a pig." (11:22) Doesn't make sense.

I have not achieved all wisdom, but now, when I find myself experiencing similar situations, I struggle to make a different decision for a different outcome. Not gonna declare to anyone, "I got this" but rather declare, "God is invited me to wisdom and I accepted."

Once God has accomplished in me His will to be able to get passed offences and be 100% in a situation, my goal is to hold fast to that and strive for higher.

One thing I have to admit in all of this, I have never in my entire life been so very free and comfortable being alone. In fact, I search for alone time. When I look in the mirror, I smile.

What Now?
You are a child of God. You are called by His name. You belong to Him. Rest in that knowledge and be at peace.

If my people, who are called by my name, will humble themselves and pray and seek my face and turn from their wicked ways, then I will hear from heaven, and I will forgive their sin and will heal their land.
(2 Chronicles 7:14).

We are His people. Our land will be healed when we follow the instructions given us. The land can be our families, or our jobs. Our land will be what God sees fit to deliver to us and what He uses to complete us. "What God sees fit" is His will for us.

Next, determine that you will take on the armor of God, to protect yourself from the attacks of the Enemy.

The whole armor of God is not just a scripture. It is life. Never take off the helmet of salvation.

Don't leave home without it. Ask those in your life, "Got salvation?"

Mother Kat said it this way: "Don't ever not be saved."

Peace on your feet. Most people know what it is like to be around people raising hell. Don't be one of them. If no one else has peace, that does not have to affect you. Everywhere you walk, you can have peace on your feet. And if the area you are in is not peaceful, take your peace with you to another area.

Righteousness on your chest. The least we can be is right. Even in the little things we think and do, we will be judged or rewarded for. When we are called by His Name, we will be rewarded crowns. In heaven, the elders laid their crown at the foot of the throne (Revelation 4:10).

If I am to lay my crown at the foot of the throne with the elders, my actions and life on earth must proclaim godliness. How sad it would be to have no crown to cast before Christ, no rewards for my works. Being right before God includes those little things.

Truth belt. Everything comes before God. We speak the truth, and we know the truth. The truth is what sets us free and when we speak it to others they can also be free.

Shield of faith. We have to believe God for everything. We must choose to trust His will for us, not our will. Then, we will have the strength to block stuff that is not for us. The shield when used correctly saved many lives. The shield blocked arrows and swords that would have otherwise pieced one thoroughly to his demise.

Many in battle trusted the shield to do its job when it was used appropriately. Hebrew Lexicon describes faith as "sure, a strong pillar that supports, given in a set amount, truth and firm (page 171)". If the shield be the faith then victory be the outcome.

Sword of God. Reading and understanding the Word of God will help us keep our mind. The Wind (Spirit) of God inspired men to write the bible. The fear of the Lord is the beginning of wisdom. It is wise to derive faith through the reading and understanding of God's word referred to as the Sword.

SPIRIT-BODY-SOUL

Our spirit has to connect with the Spirit of God and He will live in us when we are called by His Name.

And hope does not put us to shame, because God's love has been poured out into our hearts through the Holy Spirit, who has been given to us. (Romans 5:5).

In the same way, the Spirit helps us in our weakness. (Romans 8:26)

...who has set his seal of ownership on us, and put his Spirit in our hearts as a deposit, guaranteeing what is to come. (2 Corinthians 1:22).

The one who keeps God's commands lives in him, and he in them. And this is how we know that he lives in us: We know it by the Spirit he gave us. (1 John 3:24)

And the grace of our Lord was exceeding abundant with faith and love which is in Christ Jesus. (1 Tim. 1:14)

Guard the good deposit that was entrusted to you—guard it with the help of the Holy Spirit who lives in us. The Holy Spirit of God leads us to the truth. He will show us how to live when we are called by His Name

Howbeit when He, the Spirit of truth, is come, he will guide you into all truth: for He shall not speak of

himself; but whatsoever He shall hear, that shall He speak: and he will show you things to come.
(John 16:13)

The body will follow whatever part is strongest: spirit or soul. We must determine that the Spirit of God is strongest in our lives. We do this by putting on the whole armor of God, and by enabling the Holy Spirit to take control of our lives. Our will must be subjected to the will of God.

That he no longer should live the rest of his time in the flesh to the lusts of men, but to the will of God.
(1 Peter 4:2)

PHYSICAL HEALTH

Our bodies have strong wills. We don't want to exercise; we want to eat. We want to fit in with the popular cliques. I want, I want, I want. Usually when I want, I get.

What does God want for me in this body?

We must take this one step at a time. For starters, how can I serve Him in poor health? Do I need to fast? What is calling the shots in my flesh? Do I have to have my coffee every morning? What will happen if I don't have my coffee?

Do the "lusts of my flesh" rule my body? What is it that I do in private that I would not do if Jesus were standing right here?

A healthy body is a balanced body. One that is balanced with rest, food, water, and exercise.

Ask yourself, "Does my body control me to a point of being unhealthy?" If so, take steps to regain a positive balance. Consult with a doctor, a health-minded friend, or a trainer if you need assistance.

SPIRITUAL HEALTH

The health of our soul and spirit is every bit as important as the health of the body. In some ways, it is more important, because the physical body is only a temporary dwelling place for the eternal spirit, which will abide with Christ forever.

The spirit also needs to maintain a proper balance, and receive nourishment every day through the reading of God's Word, prayer, and fellowship with other believers. What I feel is also very important to God. Our feelings and emotional health are vital if we are to do our best to make a positive difference in the world and live out the purpose for which God created us.

Closing
We Are Survivors

*For I know the plans I have for you," declares
the Lord, "plans to prosper you and not to harm you,
plans to give you hope and a future.
(Jeremiah 29:11)*

Today, we are given an important choice. Will we choose to put in the work required so that we may be free? This decision requires us to also free our abusers through the act of forgiveness.

To be upset, to be mad, and to hate our abusers not only imprisons them, but it imprisons us. Often, our abusers want to be saved but they cannot forget what they have done. They cannot forgive themselves for what they did to us. Can we be strong enough to claim the freedom of forgiveness?

What is freedom? It is the ability to love without limits—anybody, anytime, anywhere.

Assignment:

- ***Who is your abuser?***

Take a piece of paper. As you write your abuser's name on a piece of paper, consciously release that person. At the same time, release yourself from having to keep their secret any longer.

- ***Who are they to you?***

Most abusers are friends, relatives, and people we had trusted. Adults are wrong to molest, fondle, and or have intercourse with minors. It is wrong morally. It is also illegal.

Children are not equipped to give such consent, and when we are hurt as children, we feel that we did something wrong. As a child, we had done nothing wrong. We have no reason to be ashamed. We will no longer be ashamed.

- ***What did the abuser do to you?***

Write it on the paper, and then tell yourself that person is, or was, sick. You did nothing wrong. They should be ashamed. They are guilty.

- ***Write over that name and over that abuse:***

"No guilt! No shame! I have done nothing wrong. This will not be a part of my future."

Closing: We are Survivors

Matthew 6:34 states, "Take therefore no thought for the morrow: for the morrow shall take thought for the things of itself. Sufficient unto the day is the evil thereof." Determine that your tomorrow will no longer be soiled by the pain or the shame of abuse.

- ***Now throw your paper in the garbage!***

- ***Breathe, and say these words to yourself:***

    "I am fearfully and wonderfully made.
    I am not a mistake.
    I am worth loving.
    I love myself because God loved me first.
    He loves me well. His grace is enough."

Decide that God's grace and His love will determine the values by which you govern your life. From this foundation, you can embark on a life of purpose and personal fulfillment.

Here are some examples of governing values you might choose to make your own:

- ***Temperance:*** Don't overdo in anything. Do not partake in anything that does not glorify God.

- ***Silence:*** Avoid trifling conversations and gossip.
- ***Resolution:*** Perform what you ought, and resolve your performance without fail.
- ***Sincerity:*** Use no harmful deceit, speak according to the truth. Don't lie.
- ***Cleanliness:*** Tolerate not uncleanliness.

HOMEWORK

When we have faced abuse, sometimes the most difficult thing to do is say something good about ourselves. We find it hard to believe that there is anything lovable about us. Begin to change that perspective about yourself, because it is not true. God's Word tells us that we are fearfully and wonderfully made.

- ***Name five GOOD things about yourself***

Rules
- Each sentence must start with the word "I."
- Each point can have nothing to do with your appearance.
- The sentences cannot have anything to do with any other.

Was it difficult? Did you do it anyway? If not, please do so before moving on to the next chapter of your life. Determine to choose freedom, which often starts with our perspective of our own bodies, our own talents, and our own choices in life.

If you're still struggling, take some time to pray and ask God to help you develop a positive self-image. All He has for you is love, grace, forgiveness, and more love. Let that love flow down until it is a part of you.

The love of Christ is eternal, and I pray that it will recreate your heart, your mind, and your spirit. I pray that when you look at your past from now on, it will be through eyes of grace. I pray that when you look at your present, it will be through eyes of hope. I pray that when you consider your future, it will be with a heart of purpose, for God has great plans for your life!

Please visit www.janicemgorden.com for more information and to contact the author

About the Author

Janice M. Gorden is an entrepreneur by day and author by night. Her published works focus on spreading a powerful message about self-esteem, courage and faith. Janice believes that all of us, young and old, are capable of using this message on our life journey. Her most recent book, Lost Identity, recounts experiences of God's grace and how it holds the ability to empower women to overcome domestic abuse. It's truly an inspiration.

Janice comes from a large family and is fourth in line among 13 siblings. Throughout her life, she has served in several ministry missions whose goal was to spread God's message to all who needed enlightenment.

She has been happily married for 17 years to Charles and has nine beautiful children, seven of whom are adopted. One of the most important things to Janice and Charles is the bond in their hearts. That bond—not blood—makes them family, and all their children are loved equally. She is also the proud grandmother of 23 grandchildren and is the great-grandmother of two.

Janice holds an Associate's Degree of Nursing and has over 32 years of nursing care experience.

Her love of nursing, children, and the need to help others has led her to establish and manage two non-profit organizations:

- *Victims of Milwaukee Violence Burial Fund.* This organization provides resources to residents of Milwaukee whose family members lost their lives to violence.

- *Destani's Child Medical Daycare Services, Inc.* This organization provides pediatric skilled nursing to special-needs children in a daycare setting.

www.ingramcontent.com/pod-product-compliance
Lightning Source LLC
Chambersburg PA
CBHW060336050426
42449CB00011B/2772